A Note from the Author

The activities in this workbook will introduce students to the time-tested literature that should be an important part of the reading program in every school. The activities will provide students from grades four through eight with meaningful reading experiences, and at the same time, reinforce a wide variety of reading skills.

Clearly, such literary matters as style and flavor may be experienced only by reading the primary source—the book itself. So, obviously, reading the book is the student's first responsibility. Students should be reminded frequently that the workbook activities are no substitute for the original text.

Rather, the workbook activities have been designed to encourage the student to read the original text—that is, the actual words of the author. These motivating workbook activities are often based on sentences and paragraphs especially written to support the teaching objective of each workbook lesson. Thus, I have declined to tinker with the words of the author and leave them properly where they belong—in their pure form in the pages of the novel.

—Claudia Dutcher Tillman

Table of Contents

Author! Author! 5

The Story in Brief 6

Word Attack Skills

Changing Short Vowels 7

Supplying Long Vowels 8

Making Compounds 9

Finding Base Words 11

Listening for Syllables 12

Comprehension Skills

Following Directions 13

Classifying Word Groups 15

Classifying Words 17

Remembering Details 18

Sequencing Events 19

Getting the Main Idea 21

Determining Fact and Opinion 23

Remembering Details 25

Drawing Conclusions 27

Determining Cause and Effect 29

Discovering Meaning Through Context 31

Remembering Details 33

Understanding Special Meanings 35

Remembering Details 37

Matching Synonyms 38

Matching Antonyms 39

Study Skills

Determining Alphabetical Order 40

Determining Alphabetical Order 41

Using a Pronunciation Key 42

Using Guide Words 43

Choosing Correct Meanings 45

Making an Outline 47

Finding Facts in the Encyclopedia 49

Creative Skills

Creating a Character 50

Creating a Picture 51

Connecting Words 52

Writing a Journal Sample 53

Using Descriptive Words 54

Describing Feelings 55

Explaining Feelings 57

Optional Spelling and Vocabulary Lists 59

Supplementary Activities 61

Response Key 63

Author! Author!
SCOTT O'DELL

Scott O'Dell was born in Los Angeles on May 23, 1902. His father, Bennett Mason O'Dell, was an official for the Union Pacific Railroad.

O'Dell graduated from Long Beach Polytechnic High School. He attended Occidental College, the University of Wisconsin, and Stanford University. He also attended the University of Rome in Italy.

After he completed his schooling, O'Dell was employed in the motion picture industry for several years. He worked first as a technical director, then as a cameraman.

Later in life, O'Dell wrote articles for several West Coast periodicals. While working on a history of California, he came across a story of an Indian girl who had lived alone on an island off the California coast for eighteen years. O'Dell based his book *Island of the Blue Dolphins* on this true story. The book won the Newbery Award in 1961.

O'Dell also wrote *The King's Fifth* and *The Black Pearl*, both runners-up for the prestigious Newbery Award. Other books by O'Dell include *Journey to Jericho*, *Sing Down the Moon*, and *Hill of the Hawk*.

The Story in Brief

Island of the Blue Dolphins is set on the island of San Nicolas, off the coast of California. The book tells of the Indian girl Karana's life from 1835 to 1853.

The story begins with a ship of Aleuts arriving at the Island of the Blue Dolphins to hunt sea otters. Following an argument with Karana's people, the Aleuts kill most of the adult tribesmen.

Several months later, a ship arrives to take the remaining Indians to another island. Ramo, Karana's brother, is accidently left behind when the ship sets sail. Karana jumps overboard and swims back to the island to be with her brother. The ship sails away, leaving the two children to fend for themselves. Ramo is later killed by a pack of wild dogs, and Karana is left alone.

Karana tries once to escape, but a canoe leak forces her to return. Knowing she cannot escape, Karana sets about making a life for herself on the island.

Karana spends her days looking for food, making weapons, and building a shelter. She finds and nurses a wounded wild dog, and he becomes her constant companion. She also befriends a young sea otter and numerous birds.

Years later, Karana finally leaves her beloved island aboard a white man's ship.

ISLAND OF THE BLUE DOLPHINS

Chapter One

Changing Short Vowels

Read each sentence. Then look at the word that comes after each sentence. Change the vowel in the word to form a new word that will make sense in the sentence. Write the new word on the blank in the sentence.

Example: The ship looked like a ____*gull*____ with folded wings.   gill

1. The ship had two _____ sails.   rod

2. Ramo was small for one who had lived so many _____ and moons.   sins

3. Karana did _____ want Ramo to run off.   nut

4. Karana dug in the _____ with a pointed stick.   brash

5. Ramo's eyes were large and _____ .   block

6. Ramo went _____ through the brush.   crushing

7. Ramo saw a _____ ship nearing the island.   bag

8. Karana _____ for roots.   dog

9. Two large _____ guarded Coral Cove.   racks

10. The _____ on the beach was white.   send

11. Forty _____ sailed on the Russian ship.   man

12. The captain took two _____ steps.   lung

13. A light _____ blew that morning.   wand

14. Karana _____ the bushes and ran home.   lift

15. The tall _____ had a yellow beard.   men

Supplying Long Vowels

One word in each of the following sentences is missing a vowel. Read each sentence. Put a vowel in each blank to form a word that will make sense in the sentence.

Example: The canyon w _*i*_ nds down to a small harbor.

1. The red ship had two red s ____ ils.

2. The sea was as smooth as a st ____ ne.

3. Karana ____ sed a stick to dig for roots.

4. There were no w ____ ves on the sea that day.

5. Ramo l ____ ked to pretend one thing was another.

6. The ship looked like a h ____ ge canoe.

7. Ramo knew what a gr ____ y whale looked like.

8. The men waited on the b ____ ach.

9. The villagers stood at the foot of the tr ____ il.

10. Karana watched from the cliff above the c ____ ve.

11. The t ____ de was out when the strangers came ashore.

12. The captain made a strange sound in his thr ____ at.

13. Everyone in the tr ____ be had two names.

14. The Russians came to hunt s ____ a otters.

15. The men from the ship came in p ____ ace.

PORTALS TO READING

Reading Skills Through Literature

ISLAND OF THE BLUE DOLPHINS

Scott O'Dell

Reproducible Activity Book
by
Claudia Dutcher Tillman

ISLAND OF THE BLUE DOLPHINS

Making Compounds

Two words combined form a compound. Each word in Box A forms the first part of a compound. Each word in Box B forms the second part. In the blank in each sentence below, write the compound that best completes the sentence. Use a word from each box to make your compounds.

Box A	
shore	north
spear	sea
~~sun~~	break
eye	every
shell	after
fire	

Box B	
one	brows
fast	heads
west	~~rise~~
light	fish
weed	line
noon	

Example: Captain Orlov moved to the island in the morning before _**sunrise**_ .

1. Sometimes the wind blew from the _____ , sometimes from the south.

2. Karana's father warned _____ in the village to stay away from the Aleuts.

3. Ulape dropped a basket full of _____ .

4. The bass tried to escape the killer whales by swimming toward the _____ .

5. Ulape discovered the fish one stormy _____ .

(continued)

Making Compounds

Chapter Two

6. The men used _____ to light their campfires.

7. The short Aleut had small eyes beneath bushy _____ .

8. The women cooked _____ over the fire.

9. Two men sharpened their _____ in preparation for the hunt.

10. That night, older men told stories by the flickering _____ .

ISLAND OF THE BLUE DOLPHINS

Chapter Two

Finding Base Words

Each word below has been formed by adding a suffix such as *ly*, *ed*, or *ing* to a base word. On the blank beside each word, write the base word.

Example: hunters _hunt_____

1. higher	_____	11. wives	_____
2. making	_____	12. settled	_____
3. camped	_____	13. stories	_____
4. pursued	_____	14. echoing	_____
5. rocky	_____	15. tried	_____
6. rejoicing	_____	16. swimming	_____
7. obeyed	_____	17. replied	_____
8. watching	_____	18. dropped	_____
9. older	_____	19. glistening	_____
10. dressed	_____	20. dried	_____

ISLAND OF THE BLUE DOLPHINS

Listening for Syllables

Say each of the words listed below to yourself. The number of vowel sounds you hear in each word will be the same as the number of syllables. Decide how many syllables are in each word. Then write the number on the blank after each word.

Example: island __*2*__

1. hunters	_____		16. beach	_____
2. flooded	_____		17. higher	_____
3. village	_____		18. league	_____
4. dolphin	_____		19. language	_____
5. profit	_____		20. older	_____
6. village	_____		21. season	_____
7. harvested	_____		22. autumn	_____
8. fortune	_____		23. echoing	_____
9. terror	_____		24. arriving	_____
10. gathered	_____		25. shore	_____
11. flopped	_____		26. cliff	_____
12. Aleuts	_____		27. enough	_____
13. pebbles	_____		28. companion	_____
14. rejoicing	_____		29. brought	_____
15. dunes	_____		30. curious	_____

Following Directions

Below is a drawing of the Island of the Blue Dolphins. Carefully read the paragraphs at the bottom of the page. Then locate on the drawing each of the places underlined in the paragraphs. Write the name of each place on the correct blank.

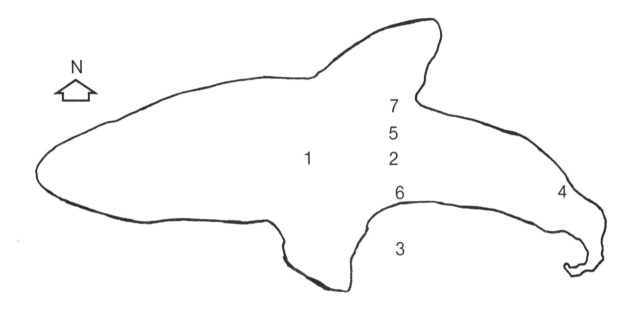

The island was shaped like a great fish sunning itself in the sea. Several <u>hills</u> rose above the island's center. Directly to the east of these hills was the village of <u>Ghalas-at</u>. North of the village was the Aleuts' <u>campground</u>. A <u>sand dune</u> separated the village from the camp.

South of the village were the <u>cliffs</u>. Below the cliffs was <u>Coral Cove</u>, guarded at its entrance by two huge rocks. Along the island's eastern coast were many <u>caves</u>.

1. _____
2. _____
3. _____
4. _____
5. _____
6. _____
7. _____

Classifying Word Groups

Read the following sentences. Decide if the italicized part of the sentence tells you *where*, *when*, or *how*. Underline the correct choice.

Example: There were kelp beds all *around the island.*   <u>where</u>   when   how

1. The Aleuts left the shore *at dawn.*   where   when   how

2. Otters played *in the beds of kelp.*   where   when   how

3. The Aleuts returned *later that night.*   where   when   how

4. Karana watched *carefully* from the cliff.   where   when   how

5. *In the morning*, the sea was red with blood.   where   when   how

6. The Aleuts skinned the animals *quickly.*   where   when   how

7. The tribesmen went *to the cliff* to count the otters.   where   when   how

8. Karana talked with her father *one morning.*   where   when   how

9. No trees grew *on the island.*   where   when   how

10. The men worked *in the cove.*   where   when   how

11. Someone checked the Russians *every hour*.   where   when   how

12. Karana looked *intently* at her father.   where   when   how

13. Logs were usually carried *to the village*.   where   when   how

14. The men labored *rapidly* by the firelight.   where   when   how

15. Karana liked the thought of beads *around her neck*.   where   when   how

16. *Next week*, the hunters would be gone.   where   when   how

17. The men slept by the log *during the night*.   where   when   how

18. The log drifted *near the shore*.   where   when   how

19. Karana peered over the cliff *cautiously*.   where   when   how

20. *During the afternoon*, the woman cleaned her aprons.   where   when   how

Classifying Words

In each group of words below, one word does not belong with the others. Draw a line through the word that does not belong.

Example: morning ~~sun~~ afternoon evening

1. tide   sea   tree   waves

2. tent   otter   dolphin   bass

3. hill   ledge   cliff   far

4. boat   rock   ship   canoe

5. watch   look   shore   stare

6. chest   hunt   fish   trap

7. pelt   fur   skin   fingers

8. foot   knee   step   ankle

9. spear   back   gun   knife

10. smile   frown   grin   win

11. line   shore   sand   beach

12. run   walk   smile   trot

13. scream   battle   cry   wail

14. hand   wrist   elbow   noise

15. animal   fish   grass   bird

16. clouds   ran   thunder   rain

17. burn   sad   happy   angry

18. quiet   still   food   silent

19. sun   star   moon   island

20. rest   men   nap   sleep

Chapter Five

Remembering Details

The following questions are about some of the characters and events in the book. Write the answers on the lines after the questions. Be sure to use complete sentences.

1. How many men of Karana's tribe survived the fight with the Aleuts? _____

_____

2. How many old men survived? _____

_____

3. Where did the villagers bury their dead? _____

_____

4. Who was chosen as the new chief of Ghalas-at? _____

_____

5. What task did Kimki assign Karana and Ulape? _____

_____

6. Why were the wild dogs a problem for the villagers? _____

_____

7. What did Kimki do in the spring? _____

_____

ISLAND OF THE BLUE DOLPHINS

Chapter Six

Sequencing Events

The events listed below are arranged in incorrect sequence. Write *1* in the blank before the event that happened first, *2* before the event that happened next, and so on.

_____ A tribesman shouted, "The Aleuts! The Aleuts!"

_____ The villagers put food and water in canoes.

_____ Nanko brought good news to the villagers.

_____ The villagers left for the hidden canoes.

_____ Matasaip told the villagers to pack their belongings.

_____ The villagers followed Nanko to the white man's ship.

_____ Matasaip went back to check the ship.

_____ The villagers were overtaken by a man with a message for Matasaip.

Getting the Main Idea

Read each of the following paragraphs. Then read the four sentences below each paragraph. Choose the sentence that best states the main idea of the paragraph. Then neatly copy that sentence on the line provided.

a. Karana filled two baskets with things she wished to take. There were three fine needles of whalebone, an awl for making holes, and a good stone knife for scraping hides. She also took two cooking pots and a small box made from a shell.

1. Karana liked to sew.
2. The villagers had plenty of baskets.
3. Karana needed pots for cooking.
4. Karana packed her belongings into baskets.

b. Karana called to her brother. She knew he was very curious, and, therefore, would be in the way of the men who were working. The wind drowned her voice, and Ramo did not answer. The deck was very crowded, but Karana pushed her way from one end of the ship to the other, calling Ramo's name. Ramo still did not answer.

1. Karana searched for Ramo on the ship.
2. The ship was crowded.
3. The wind bothered Karana.
4. Ramo was curious.

(continued)

Getting the Main Idea

Chapter Seven

c.   The ship was anchored outside the cove. Nanko said that the ship could not come closer to shore because of the high waves. The waves beat against the rocks with the sound of thunder. As far as Karana could see, the shore was rimmed with foam.

1. High waves kept the ship away from shore.
2. Nanko told the sailors to move the ship.
3. The ship beat against the rocks.
4. Nanko dropped the ship's anchor.

---

d.   The ship was large, many times the size of the islanders' biggest canoes. Two tall masts with beautiful sails towered over the ship's deck.

1. The ship was the size of a big canoe.
2. The large ship had tall masts with beautiful sails.
3. The ship was faster than a canoe.
4. The masts were larger than a canoe.

Determining Fact and Opinion

Some of the following sentences are statements of fact. Some are statements of opinion. In the blank before each sentence, write the letter *F* if that sentence is a statement of fact. Write *O* if that sentence is a statement of opinion.

Example: __*F*__ Ramo and Karana took shelter among the rocks.

_____ 1. Wild dogs ate most of the abandoned food.

_____ 2. Wild dogs are beautiful animals.

_____ 3. Karana cooked on a flat rock.

_____ 4. Ramo caught fish in a small pool.

_____ 5. Gull eggs are delicious.

_____ 6. Cooking on a flat rock is easy.

_____ 7. Karana wove a basket from seaweed.

_____ 8. Seaweed baskets are lovely.

_____ 9. A string of sea-elephant teeth makes a wonderful necklace.

_____ 10. Ramo was the son of Chowig.

(continued)

Determining Fact and Opinion

Chapter Eight

_____ 11. Living on an island can be dangerous.

_____ 12. Ramo was too young to pass the rites of manhood.

_____ 13. Ramo called himself Chief Tanyositlopai.

_____ 14. Karana hid the shellfish in a hole.

_____ 15. Karana gathered mussels from the rocks.

_____ 16. Hunting for mussels is hard work.

_____ 17. Ramo had a deep wound in his throat.

_____ 18. People should not be afraid of wild dogs.

_____ 19. Karana chased the wild dogs into a cave.

_____ 20. Karana vowed she would kill all the wild dogs.

ISLAND OF THE BLUE DOLPHINS

Chapter Nine

Remembering Details

The following questions are about some of the characters and events in the book. Write the answers on the lines after questions. Be sure to use complete sentences.

1. What happened to the huts in the village? _____

_____

2. Why did Karana sleep on a rock? _____

_____

3. Why was Karana afraid to make weapons? _____

_____

4. Where did Karana find the chest? _____

_____

5. What was in the chest? _____

_____

6. What did Karana throw into the sea? _____

_____

7. What did Karana use for a spearhead? _____

_____

8. What did Karana use for a bed? _____

_____

Chapter Ten

Drawing Conclusions

In each of the following paragraphs, an item is described but not named. Read each paragraph and decide what is being described. Write your answers on the blank after each question.

1. Karana watched the small object in the distance. She thought the object was a ship, but then a stream of water rose from it.

    What did Karana see? _____

2. Karana carefully slid it into the water. She was not very skilled in handling it, but she was determined. She knelt in the middle of it and paddled hard.

    What did Karana slide in the water? _____

3. Karana watched it appear in the night sky overhead. It twinkled brightly. Karana kept her gaze upon it. Without it, Karana would lose her way in the dark sea.

    What did Karana watch? _____

(continued)

Drawing Conclusions

Chapter Ten

4. Water seeped in whenever the canoe rose and fell. Karana tore pieces of it. She stuffed the fiber into the crack.

   What did Karana tear? _____

5. They came and stood outside the ring made by the fire. Karana saw their eyes gleaming in the dark and heard their growls. She killed three of them with arrows.

   What did Karana kill? _____

6. They swam beside the canoe, so close that Karana could see their eyes and broad snouts. They were animals of good omen. Karana was glad to have them near.

   What animals swam by Karana's canoe? _____

Chapter Eleven

Determining Cause and Effect

To determine a cause, ask "What is the reason?" To determine an effect, ask "What is the result?" Match the causes and effects below. Write the number of the cause in front of its effect.

Cause	Effect
1. Karana needed plenty of fresh water.	_____ Karana turned the canoe over.
2. Karana was exhausted from her trip in the canoe.	_____ Karana did not go near the village.
3. Karana did not want the tides to take the canoe out to sea.	_____ Karana had little time to waste.
4. Karana needed a place to live.	_____ The fire would not stay lit in the damp weather.
5. The storms would be coming soon.	_____ Karana looked for a place to live near a spring.
6. The sea elephants were very noisy.	_____ Karana did not build a shelter near them.
7. Karana wanted to forget the people who were gone.	_____ Karana needed to build a fence.
8. The rain fell for two days.	_____ Karana searched the island for a good location.
9. Karana could not build a fire.	_____ Karana fell asleep on the sand.
10. The red foxes on the island were clever thieves.	_____ Karana was very cold.

Discovering Meaning Through Context

Read the following sentences. Three meanings are given for each italicized word. Use the context of the sentence to figure out which meaning is correct. Circle the correct meaning.

Example: The water near the headland had a *brackish* taste.

   muddy   salty   (bitter)

1. Karana found some seeds in a *ravine*.

   canyon   cave   hut

2. The sea elephants' *clamor* was deafening.

   call   song   uproar

3. After three wet days, the rain finally *ceased*.

   slowed   stopped   started

4. The otter played in the *kelp*.

   seaweed   ocean   tide

5. Karana considered the clear, fresh morning a good *omen*.

   food   beginning   sign

(continued)

Chapter Eleven

6. Water *seeped* through the crack in the canoe.

       gushed   disappeared   leaked

7. The foxes were too *numerous* for Karana to destroy them all.

       noisy   many   mean

8. Sweet *odors* came from the wild grasses in the ravines.

       berries   smells   flowers

9. The headland seemed the more *favorable* of the two locations.

       promising   difficult   colorful

10. Karana needed a place that was *sheltered* from the wind.

       exposed   harmed   protected

ISLAND OF THE BLUE DOLPHINS

Chapter Twelve

Remembering Details

To work the puzzle, use the words that complete the sentences below.

Across

2. Karana built a house on the ____ .
5. Karana blew on the ____ to start the fire.
6. ____ lived alone on the island.
7. Karana needed a bull elephant's tooth. to finish her ____ .
8. Karana's ancestors had cut figures in the ____ of the cave.
10. The tribesmen used a ____ to catch the bull sea elephant.
11. The fence was made of whale ____ .
13. Karana made ____ from dried fish.
14. ____ leaves covered the roof.
15. The island's ____ were stunted.

Down

1. Karana wove a ____ out of fine reeds.
3. Karana made a bow and ____ .
4. Karana planned to kill the wild ____ .
5. Karana doubted that she could kill a bull sea ____ with an arrow or spear.
9. An old ____ said tall trees once grew on the island.
12. The villagers made ornaments out of whale ____ .

Understanding Special Meanings

Read the following sentences. Explain in your own words the meaning of the italicized word or group of words. Write your response on the line below each sentence.

Example: The bulls sat *like great gray boulders* on the pebbly shore.

*huge, gray, and still*

1. Karana worried that one of the bulls might *turn on her*.

_____

2. The bull's skin looked *like wet earth that had dried in the sun and cracked.*

_____

3. Karana tried not to *put the sea elephants on their guard.*

_____

4. The bulls *sat like great chiefs* watching their herds.

_____

(continued)

Understanding
Special Meanings

Chapter Thirteen

5. Karana *took pains* not to send stones tumbling down the slope.

_____

6. The old bull and the young bull were *locked together*.

_____

7. The young bull's eyes *shone fiercely red*.

_____

8. The old bull *bore down* upon the younger one.

_____

9. The old bull went over the cows in his path *as if they were small stones*.

_____

Chapter Fourteen

Remembering Details

The following questions are about some of the characters and events in the book. Write the answers on the lines after the questions. Be sure to use complete sentences.

1. Why did Karana stay in her house for five days? _____

_____

2. Why did she finally leave? _____

_____

3. Why did Karana leave her bow and arrows behind? _____

_____

4. Where did Karana stay after she left the spring? _____

_____

5. How long did she stay there? _____

_____

6. What had been cut into the walls of the cave? _____

_____

7. What did Karana find when the tide was low? _____

_____

Name _____

Chapter Fifteen

Matching Synonyms

A synonym is a word having the same or nearly the same meaning as another word. Choose a synonym for each word in the Word List. Write the synonym on the blank.

Word List		**Synonym**
Example: big	_large_	smell
1. begin	_____	hit
2. sound	_____	steps
3. wise	_____	scare
4. sniff	_____	killed
5. quiver	_____	ridge
6. frighten	_____	start
7. spring	_____	smart
8. slain	_____	fix
9. struck	_____	injury
10. ledge	_____	~~large~~
11. paces	_____	jump
12. mend	_____	daybreak
13. wound	_____	grasped
14. dawn	_____	shake
15. held	_____	noise

Matching Antonyms

An antonym is a word which means the opposite or nearly the opposite of another word. Choose an antonym for each word in the Word List. Write the antonym on the blank.

	Word List		**Antonym**
Example:	front	_back_	late
1.	first	_____	tame
2.	young	_____	outside
3.	wild	_____	wide
4.	early	_____	last
5.	many	_____	thick
6.	inside	_____	lower
7.	leave	_____	friend
8.	raise	_____	noisily
9.	close	_____	old
10.	enemy	_____	few
11.	thin	_____	found
12.	quietly	_____	evening
13.	lost	_____	~~back~~
14.	narrow	_____	far
15.	morning	_____	come

Chapter Sixteen

Determining Alphabetical Order

Words are listed in a dictionary in alphabetical order. Number the six words in each list below to show the order in which they would appear in a dictionary. Write *1* on the blank before the word that comes first alphabetically, and so on.

Example:

_5_	summer
_4_	spring
_1_	shellfish
_6_	sure
_3_	spit
_2_	since

A.

_____	Aleut
_____	brush
_____	black
_____	also
_____	barking
_____	all

B.

_____	look
_____	labored
_____	leak
_____	learned
_____	knives
_____	lonely

C.

_____	rains
_____	paid
_____	ring
_____	others
_____	path
_____	roof

D.

_____	upon
_____	when
_____	with
_____	whined
_____	understand
_____	winter

E.

_____	came
_____	catch
_____	down
_____	climb
_____	dress
_____	cliff

F.

_____	night
_____	memories
_____	many
_____	out
_____	over
_____	nearly

G.

_____	grass
_____	fashioning
_____	great
_____	house
_____	headland
_____	floor

H.

_____	storms
_____	raised
_____	spear
_____	reach
_____	rest
_____	short

Chapter Seventeen

Determining Alphabetical Order

Most of the words in the list below are in alphabetical order. However, some of the words have either jumped ahead or fallen back. Cross out the words that are too far ahead or too far back. The remaining words will then be in alphabetical order. Complete the Word-Search Puzzle by hunting down the correctly alphabetized words.

arrows
bow
together
canoe
devilfish
errors
mound
flight
happy
warily
large
memories
noise
attacker
paused
quiet
divided
ravine
strangely
lifted
teeth
trotting
crouching
whined
wound

Word-Search Puzzle

```
A  D  B  G  N  I  T  T  O  R  T  B
S  E  D  C  T  O  E  F  I  G  O  H
T  S  N  P  H  E  I  J  M  W  K  L
R  U  Q  O  G  R  I  S  O  H  W  S
A  A  U  T  I  S  V  U  E  I  Y  E
N  P  V  Z  L  E  N  X  Q  N  T  I
G  A  B  I  F  D  O  C  D  E  E  R
E  I  H  G  N  F  E  N  E  D  R  O
L  A  R  G  E  E  K  T  A  M  R  M
Y  J  Y  P  P  A  H  L  N  C  O  E
R  T  S  Q  S  W  O  R  R  A  R  M
D  E  V  I  L  F  I  S  H  O  S  P
```

Chapter Eighteen

Using a Pronunciation Key

Use the key at the bottom of the page to help pronounce the respelled words. Write the word correctly spelled on the line beside the Respelled Word. Use the Word List to help figure out the Respelled Word.

Respelled Word		Word List
Example: (rēth)	*wreath*	cage
1. (klus′ tər)	_____	ravine
2. (sinj)	_____	quarrel
3. (fas′ ′n)	_____	speckled
4. (krev′ is)	_____	island
5. (flou′ ər)	_____	because
6. (rə vēn′)	_____	fasten
7. (skär′ lit)	_____	crevice
8. (kāj)	_____	~~wreath~~
9. (spek′ ′ld)	_____	together
10. (ī′ lənd)	_____	away
11. (kwôr′ əl)	_____	flower
12. (ə wā′)	_____	cluster
13. (bi kôz′)	_____	singe
14. (tə geth′ ər)	_____	scarlet

pat/ cāke/ cär/ pet/ mē/ **i**t/ nīce/ pot/ cōld/ nôrth/
book/ fo͞ol/ boil/ **out**/ cup/ mūle/ bu**r**n/ si**ng**/ **th**in/
*th*is/ hw in **wh**ite/ zh in plea**s**ure/ ə in **a**bout
The ′ mark indicates an accented syllable.

Chapter Nineteen

Using Guide Words

At the top of each dictionary page are guide words. These words are the first and last words on a dictionary page. The other words on the page fall in alphabetical order between the guide words.

Put the boxed words below in alphabetical order under the correct guide words. One has been done for you.

giant	beaks	swim
dolphins	throwing	gold
moving	knife	clear
few	string	leeches
sand	black	many
fish	~~arms~~	rocks

act—fin	final—march	mare—tongue
1. *arms*	1. _____	1. _____
2. _____	2. _____	2. _____
3. _____	3. _____	3. _____
4. _____	4. _____	4. _____
5. _____	5. _____	5. _____
6. _____	6. _____	6. _____

Choosing Correct Meanings

The italicized word in each of the sentences below has several meanings. The meanings are listed in the Glossary. Decide which meaning the word has in the sentence. Then write the number of your choice on the blank.

Glossary

back 1. part of the body behind the chest 2. to or toward a former condition 3. of or for the past

hold 1. to keep in a certain position 2. to contain 3. to take part in 4. a grasp

look 1. to see 2. to search 3. to appear or seem

pitch 1. to toss 2. to set up 3. to fall forward 4. a throw to a batter (in baseball) 5. sticky substance made from tar

plant 1. vegetation such as bushes or flowers 2. to set in the ground 3. to place firmly in position

spring 1. to jump quickly 2. place where water comes up from underground 3. season between winter and summer

Example: ____/____ Karana covered her *back* with cormorant skins.

_____ 1. Karana lined her basket with *pitch*.

_____ 2. Karana had a tight *hold* on the string.

_____ 3. Karana ate the roots of *plants*.

_____ 4. One cloud *looked* different from all others.

_____ 5. The *spring* weather was lovely that year.

(continued)

Choosing Correct Meanings

Chapter Twenty

_____ 6. Karana *looked* for abalones.

_____ 7. Karana gently patted Rontu's *back*.

_____ 8. Karana *pitched* the shells over the cliff.

_____ 9. The cave stood close to the *spring*.

_____ 10. Karana went *back* to the cave.

_____ 11. The devilfish would not *hold* still.

_____ 12. Karana *looked* around the island for a straight pole.

_____ 13. Karana *planted* her feet firmly on the sand.

_____ 14. The Aleuts *pitched* tents on the sand.

_____ 15. Karana used a basket to *hold* water.

ISLAND OF THE BLUE DOLPHINS

Making an Outline

Read the article below. Think about the topics and subtopics of each paragraph. Use the Word List provided to outline the article. The topics should come after the numerals. The subtopics come after the capital letters. List the topics and subtopics in the order the items fall in the article.

Part of the outline has been done for you. Be sure to capitalize the first letter of the topics and subtopics.

Ocean Life

Plankton are plants and animals that float or drift about in ocean waters. One common plankton is the diatom, a basic food supply for many fish. Other plankton are copepods, jellyfish, radiolarians, and arrowworms.

Animals that swim about freely in the ocean are called nekton. Some of these animals, such as dolphins and sailfish, can swim very fast. Also in this group are whales, squid, and seals.

Benthos are plants and animals that live on or near the ocean bottoms. Seaweed, one of the benthos group, grows in shallow water or along the shore. Starfish and sponges are benthos that live on the ocean bottom. Oysters and corals also live on the sea floor.

(continued)

Making an Outline

Chapter Twenty-One

Ocean Life

I. _Plankton_

    A. _____

    B. _____

    C. _____

    D. _____

    E. _____

II. _____

    A. _Dolphins_

    B. _____

    C. _____

    D. _____

    E. _____

III. _____

    A. _____

    B. _Starfish_

    C. _____

    D. _____

    E. _____

Word List

Seals

Sailfish

Diatoms

Seaweed

Corals

Squid

~~Plankton~~

Radiolarians

Sponges

Whales

~~Starfish~~

~~Ocean Life~~

Arrowworms

Nekton

Jellyfish

Oysters

Copepods

Benthos

~~Dolphins~~

Chapter Twenty-Two

Finding Facts in the Encyclopedia

A sample encyclopedia set is drawn below. Imagine that you need these volumes of the encyclopedia to respond to the questions below. Circle the word or words in each question that might help you find the answers.

Use the circled words to decide which volume or volumes you will need to answer each question. Write the volume number or numbers on the blank.

A	B	C-Ch	Ci-Cz	D	E	F	G	H	I	J-K	L	M	N-O	P	Q-R	S-Sn	So-Sz	T	U-V	W X YZ
1	2	3	4	5	6	7	8	9	10	11	12	13	14	15	16	17	18	19	20	21

Example: ____*12*____ How long is a (league)?

_____ 1. How does an abalone cling to a rock?

_____ 2. How do dolphins locate underwater objects?

_____ 3. What color are most gulls?

_____ 4. What is a cormorant?

_____ 5. Which mussels can be eaten?

_____ 6. What do otters eat?

_____ 7. How many different types of islands are there?

_____ 8. What causes tides?

_____ 9. Is seaweed edible?

_____ 10. What color are the flowers on a lupine plant?

ISLAND OF THE BLUE DOLPHINS

Chapter Twenty-Three

Creating a Character

Imagine you are a villager living on the Island of the Blue Dolphins. You are being interviewed by a newspaper reporter. Write your responses to the reporter's questions on the lines provided. Be sure to use complete sentences.

Reporter: What do you find to eat on this island?

Villager: _____

_____

Reporter: Are there any dangerous animals on the island?

Villager: _____

_____

Reporter: Are there other villages on the island?

Villager: _____

_____

Reporter: What do you do for fun on the island?

Villager: _____

_____

Reporter: What do you like best about living on an island?

Villager: _____

_____

Creating a Picture

Draw one of the scenes the author describes in Chapter Twenty-Four. Then write your own description of what you have drawn. Be sure to use complete sentences.

_____

_____

ISLAND OF THE BLUE DOLPHINS

Chapter Twenty-Five

Connecting Words

Look at the three words in each set below. Combine the words to form a sentence that expresses a complete thought. Write the sentence on the line after each group of words.

Example: spring/shellfish/dried *Karana dried shellfish every spring.*

1. spear/bow/arrows _____

2. hunters/summer/watched _____

3. herd/otter/cave _____

4. high/cliff/gulls _____

5. dog/tracks/alone _____

6. dawn/light/sky _____

7. bark/night/sound _____

8. dug/buried/rock _____

9. canoe/island/stored _____

10. stored/weapons/hunters _____

11. fish/moons/reef _____

12. dunes/hill/lair _____

13. beat/heart/hollow _____

14. crevice/pebbles/hole _____

15. lie/house/sun _____

Writing a Journal Sample

Imagine that you are Karana. In the sample journal below, describe how you captured and tamed Rontu-Aru. Be sure to use complete sentences.

Character _____

○	
○	

ISLAND OF THE BLUE DOLPHINS

Chapter Twenty-Seven

Using Descriptive Words

List seven words that can be used to describe each of the italicized words below. Be creative. Write your words on the blanks.

Example: *ghost*

1. _pale_
2. _spooky_
3. _mischievous_
4. _floating_
5. _mysterious_
6. _shimmering_
7. _friendly_

A. *otter*

1. _____
2. _____
3. _____
4. _____
5. _____
6. _____
7. _____

B. *dog*

1. _____
2. _____
3. _____
4. _____
5. _____
6. _____
7. _____

C. *sea*

1. _____
2. _____
3. _____
4. _____
5. _____
6. _____
7. _____

D. *earthquake*

1. _____
2. _____
3. _____
4. _____
5. _____
6. _____
7. _____

Describing Feelings

A person does not always express feelings directly in words. Sometimes feelings are shown through other clues as well. Each of the sentences below provides clues to the feelings of a character in the book. The name of that character is italicized. First study the clues, then choose the word from the box that best describes the character's feelings. Write the word on the blank in front of the sentence.

worried	excited	curious	afraid	contented
relieved	angry	lonely	amused	surprised

_____ 1. Everything *Karana* saw filled her with much happiness.

_____ 2. *Karana* hurriedly searched the ship when Ramo did not answer her call.

_____ 3. *Ramo* shouted and clapped his hands when he saw the huge ship with the red sails.

_____ 4. *Karana's* heart ached for her family and friends.

_____ 5. *Karana* scurried away when she saw the two sea elephants come rushing toward her.

_____ 6. *Karana* chuckled quietly at the sight of the sea-elephant teeth around Ramo's neck.

_____ 7. *Karana* wondered how the necklace would look around her neck.

_____ 8. When she reached the shore safe and sound, *Karana* hugged the sand of her beloved island.

_____ 9. "The dogs have killed my brother," *Karana* cried. "I will kill them!"

_____ 10. *Karana's* mouth dropped open in amazement when she saw the Aleut girl looking at her.

Explaining Feelings

The questions below ask you to describe the feelings you had as you read the book. Read each question carefully. Write your response on the lines provided. Explain why you felt the way you did. Be sure to use complete sentences.

1. How did you feel when the Aleuts slaughtered the otters?

_____

_____

_____

2. How did you feel when the Aleuts killed the men of Ghalas-at?

_____

_____

_____

3. How did you feel when the wild dogs killed Ramo?

_____

_____

_____

(continued)

Explaining Feelings

4. How did you feel when Karana's canoe started to leak?

_____

_____

_____

5. How did you feel when Rontu died?

_____

_____

_____

6. How did you feel when Karana made friends with Rontu-Aru?

_____

_____

_____

7. How did you feel when Karana was finally rescued from the island?

_____

_____

_____

Optional Spelling and Vocabulary Lists

Below are six word lists from the book. The lists can be used as spelling or vocabulary words.

Chapters 1—5

dolphins	gull
ravine	whale
weapons	canoe
island	beach
otter	tide
seaweed	reef
pelts	kelp
ledge	bass
memory	terrible
warriors	preparations

Chapters 6—10

shrouded	stout
entrance	scan
message	alarm
quantity	stern
earrings	mesa
beckoned	rough
language	spear
sheltered	cliff
reminded	bracelets
beneath	protection

Chapters 11—15

guarded	foam
harbor	ridge
elephants	search
destroyed	dune
impossible	scarce
straight	ashes
distance	rough
scars	spite
necessary	herbs
satisfied	poisonous

Optional Spelling and Vocabulary Lists

Chapters 16—20

surrounded	heavy
abandoned	dawn
loosening	drift
voyage	knelt
numerous	bulge
liquid	leak
enemy	shaft
sinew	yucca
favorable	plentiful
scallops	tightened

Chapters 21—25

league	giddy
tangled	disks
fortunate	gash
sprawled	dusk
necklace	herbs
deserted	beak
reflection	chase
especially	shore
magical	fledglings
quiver	scarcely

Chapters 26—29

notched	stride
gnawing	snare
breathe	dim
shields	crest
crevices	gleam
damage	waded
wreckage	mist
horizon	cape
ornament	gesture
scratched	beneath

Supplementary Activities

Below is a list of ideas that could be used as supplementary or culminating activities.

   I. Oral reading

      A. To the entire class

      B. To each other

      C. To the teacher

      D. To a tape recorder

  II. Group discussions

      A. Author's writing style

      B. Ideas gained from the book

      C. Parts of the book

          1. Most important

          2. Most frightening

          3. Most humorous

          4. Most saddening

          5. Most exciting

          6. Most liked

      D. Characters

          1. Did the characters seem real?

          2. What was the most admirable trait of each character?

          3. What was the least admirable trait of each character?

          4. Which character was the student's favorite? Why?

          5. List questions to ask each character.

Supplementary Activities

III. Spelling bee using words from the book

IV. Role play situations from the book

  V. Artistic creations

     A. Murals

     B. Dioramas

     C. Book jackets

     D. Posters

     E. Puppets

     F. Poetry

     G. Costumes

     H. Portraits

     I. Mobiles

     J. Songs

     K. Newspaper headlines, articles, and drawings

VI. Research

     A. Island

     B. Cave

     C. Ship

     D. Canoe

     E. Ocean life

     F. Seaweed and kelp

     G. Sea otter, sea elephant, dolphin, whale

     H. Cormorant, pelican, gull

     I. Abalone, shellfish, mussels

     J. Devilfish or octopus

VII. Read other books by the same author

Response Key

WORD ATTACK SKILLS

Changing Short Vowels (page 7)
1. red; 2. suns; 3. not; 4. brush; 5. black; 6. crashing; 7. big; 8. dug; 9. rocks; 10. sand; 11. men; 12. long; 13. wind; 14. left; 15. man.

Supplying Long Vowels (page 8)
1. sails; 2. stone; 3. used; 4. waves; 5. liked; 6. huge; 7. gray; 8. beach; 9. trail; 10. cave; 11. tide; 12. throat; 13. tribe; 14. sea; 15. peace.

Making Compounds (page 9)
1. northwest; 2. everyone; 3. shellfish; 4. shoreline; 5. afternoon; 6. seaweed; 7. eyebrows; 8. breakfast; 9. spearheads; 10. firelight.

Finding Base Words (page 11)
1. high; 2. make; 3. camp; 4. pursue; 5. rock; 6. rejoice; 7. obey; 8. watch; 9. old; 10. dress; 11. wife; 12. settle; 13. story; 14. echo; 15. try; 16. swim; 17. reply; 18. drop; 19. glisten; 20. dry.

Listening for Syllables (page 12)
1. 2; 2. 2; 3. 2; 4. 2; 5. 2; 6. 2; 7. 3; 8. 2; 9. 2; 10. 2; 11. 1; 12. 2; 13. 2; 14. 3; 15. 1; 16. 1; 17. 2; 18. 1; 19. 2; 20. 2; 21. 2; 22. 2; 23. 3; 24. 3; 25. 1; 26. 1; 27. 2; 28. 3; 29. 1; 30. 3.

COMPREHENSION SKILLS

Following Directions (page 13)
1. hills; 2. Ghalas-at; 3. Coral Cove; 4. caves; 5. sand dune; 6. cliffs; 7. campground.

Classifying Word Groups (page 15)
1. when; 2. where; 3. when; 4. how; 5. when; 6. how; 7. where; 8. when; 9. where; 10. where; 11. when; 12. how; 13. where; 14. how; 15. where; 16. when; 17. when; 18. where; 19. how; 20. when.

Classifying Words (page 17)
1. tree; 2. tent; 3. far; 4. rock; 5. shore; 6. chest; 7. fingers; 8. step; 9. back;
10. win; 11. line; 12. smile; 13. battle; 14. noise; 15. grass; 16. ran; 17. burn;
18. food; 19. island; 20. men.

Remembering Details (page 18)
1. Fifteen men survived the fight with the Aleuts. 2. Of the fifteen men who survived,
seven were old men. 3. The dead were buried on the south headland. 4. The council chose
Kimki as the new chief. 5. Karana and Ulape were given the task of gathering abalones.
6. The wild dogs came into the village to steal food. 7. In the spring, Kimki left to find
a new place for the tribe to live.

Sequencing Events (page 19)
2, 1, 7, 4, 3, 8, 6, 5.

Getting the Main Idea (page 21)
A. Karana packed her belongings into two baskets. B. Karana searched for Ramo on
the ship. C. High waves kept the ship away from shore. D. The large ship had tall masts
with beautiful sails.

Determining Fact and Opinion (page 23)
1. F; 2. O; 3. F; 4. F; 5. O; 6. O; 7. F; 8. O; 9. O; 10. F; 11. O; 12. O; 13. F; 14. F;
15. F; 16. O; 17. F; 18. O; 19. F; 20. F.

Remembering Details (page 25)
1. Karana burned the huts in the village. 2. Karana slept on a rock to protect herself
from the wild dogs. 3. The laws of Ghalas-at forbade women from making weapons.
4. Karana found the chest buried in the sand. 5. Beads, bracelets, and earrings were
in the chest. 6. Karana threw the beads, bracelets, and earrings into the sea. 7. Karana
used the root of a tree for a spearhead. 8. Karana used dry seaweed for a bed.

Drawing Conclusions (page 27)
1. a whale; 2. a canoe; 3. a star (the North Star); 4. her skirt; 5. wild dogs;
6. dolphins.

Determining Cause and Effect (page 29)
3, 7, 5, 8, 1, 6, 10, 4, 2, 9.

Discovering Meaning Through Context (page 31)
1. canyon; 2. uproar; 3. stopped; 4. seaweed; 5. sign; 6. leaked; 7. many; 8. smells; 9. promising; 10. protected.

Remembering Details (page 33)

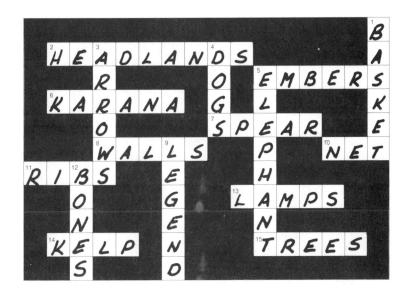

Understanding Special Meanings (page 35)
1. attack her; 2. brown and lined; 3. upset them; 4. looked dignified and in charge; 5. was careful; 6. in a fighting embrace; 7. glowed with rage; 8. approached; 9. trampled over the cows without noticing them.

Remembering Details (page 37)
1. Her leg was badly swollen. 2. Karana left because she ran out of water. 3. She left them behind because the brush was too heavy and she could not use her weapons. 4. Karana stayed in a cave. 5. She stayed there for six days. 6. Figures of animals had been cut into the walls. 7. Karana found the body of the old bull sea elephant.

Matching Synonyms (page 38)
1. start; 2. noise; 3. smart; 4. smell; 5. shake; 6. scare; 7. jump; 8. killed; 9. hit; 10. ridge; 11. steps; 12. fix; 13. injury; 14. daybreak; 15. grasped.

Matching Antonyms (page 39)
1. last; 2. old; 3. tame; 4. late; 5. few; 6. outside; 7. come; 8. lower; 9. far; 10. friend; 11. thick; 12. noisily; 13. found; 14. wide; 15. evening.

STUDY SKILLS

Determining Alphabetical Order (page 40)

A. 1, 6, 5, 3, 4, 2;
B. 6, 2, 3, 4, 1, 5;
C. 4, 2, 5, 1, 3, 6;
D. 2, 3, 6, 4, 1, 5;
E. 1, 2, 5, 4, 6, 3;
F. 4, 2, 1, 5, 6, 3;
G. 3, 1, 4, 6, 5, 2;
H. 6, 1, 5, 2, 3, 4.

Determining Alphabetical Order (page 41)

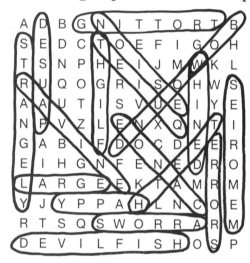

Words crossed out: together, mound, warily, attacker, divided, lifted, crouching.

Using a Pronunciation Key (page 42)

1. cluster; 2. singe; 3. fasten; 4. crevice; 5. flower; 6. ravine; 7. scarlet; 8. cage; 9. speckled; 10. island; 11. quarrel; 12. away; 13. because; 14. together.

Using Guide Words (page 43)

act—fin	final—march	mare—tongue
1. arms	1. fish	1. moving
2. beaks	2. giant	2. rocks
3. black	3. gold	3. sand
4. clear	4. knife	4. string
5. dolphins	5. leeches	5. swim
6. few	6. many	6. throwing

Choosing Correct Meanings (page 45)
1. 5; 2. 4; 3. 1; 4. 3; 5. 3; 6. 2; 7. 1; 8. 1; 9. 2; 10. 2; 11. 1; 12. 2; 13. 3; 14. 2; 15. 2.

Making an Outline (page 47)
Ocean Life
I. Plankton
    A. Diatoms
    B. Copepods
    C. Jellyfish
    D. Radiolarians
    E. Arrowworms

II. Nekton
    A. Dolphins
    B. Sailfish
    C. Whales
    D. Squid
    E. Seals

III. Benthos
    A. Seaweed
    B. Starfish
    C. Sponges
    D. Oysters
    E. Corals

Finding Facts in the Encyclopedia (page 49)
1. 1, abalone; 2. 5, dolphins; 3. 8, gulls; 4. 4, cormorant; 5. 13, mussels; 6. 14, otters;
7. 10, islands; 8. 19, tides; 9. 17, seaweed; 10. 12, lupine.

CREATIVE SKILLS

Creating a Character (page 50)
Responses will vary.

Creating a Picture (page 51)
Responses and pictures will vary.

Connecting Words (page 52)
Responses will vary.

Writing a Journal Sample (page 53)
Responses will vary.

Using Descriptive Words (page 54)
Responses will vary.

Describing Feelings (page 55)
1. contented; 2. worried; 3. excited; 4. lonely; 5. afraid; 6. amused; 7. curious; 8. relieved;
9. angry; 10. surprised.

Explaining Feelings (page 57)
Responses will vary.